Rapunzel

Level 4

Retold by Georgina Swinburne
Series Editor: Melanie Williams

Pearson Education Limited
Pearson
KAO Two
KAO Park
Harlow
Essex
CM17 9NA

and Associated Companies throughout the world.

ISBN 9781292240183

Rapunzel
Level 4

First published by Librairie du Liban Publishers, 1996
This adaptation first published by
Penguin Books 2000
3 5 7 9 10 8 6 4

Text copyright © Pearson Education Limited 2000
Illustrations copyright © 1996 Librairie du Liban

Retold by Georgina Swinburne
Series Editor: Melanie Williams
Designed by Shireen Nathoo Design
Illustrated by Jenny Press

Printed in Slovakia by Neografia

The moral right of the author and illustrator have been asserted

Published by Pearson Education Limited

For a complete list of titles available in the Pearson Story Readers series please write
to your local Pearson Education office or contact:
Pearson, KAO Two, KAO Park, Harlow, Essex, CM17 9NA

Answers for the Activities in this book are published in the free Pearson English Story
Readers Factsheet on the website, www.pearsonenglishreaders.com

Once upon a time a man and his wife lived in a little cottage beside a forest. They were poor, and sometimes they did not have enough to eat. They were going to have a baby soon, so they were very happy.

   Their neighbor was a strange old woman who never talked to them. In her garden there were a lot of vegetables, but she never gave any to the hungry man and his wife.

The man and his wife were afraid of the old woman, but they were very hungry. One night, the man went into his neighbor's garden to steal some of the vegetables. The old woman heard him, opened her door, and shouted, "Who's that?"

The man tried to explain to the old woman.

"I'm sorry. My wife and I are hungry. She needs some vegetables because she's going to have a baby," he said.

The old woman smiled cruelly. "You can take those vegetables," she said, "and when the baby is born, you must give her to me."

The man didn't know what to do. The old woman was frightening him, but he had to help his hungry wife and give her the vegetables. She needed good food.

"Yes, yes," he said to the old woman as he climbed over the wall.

The man showed the vegetables to his wife. He told her what the old woman had said.

"Don't worry!" she told him. "Nobody will take a baby away from its family. She's old; she doesn't want our baby; she just wants to frighten us. She was angry because you were in her garden taking her vegetables."

They ate the delicious vegetables and forgot what the old woman had said.

That night, the man dreamed of his new baby. In his dream, he and his wife were playing with the baby. They were all very happy together.

In the daytime, the dream frightened him. He remembered the old woman. Every day until his baby was born, he worried about what she had said.

In the summer, a baby girl was born. The happy parents had forgotten about their neighbor, until one day there was a loud knock at the door.

Knock, knock, knock!

It was the old woman! She stole the baby from them and ran away.

"No! Don't take our little baby!" the parents cried.

It was too late. The old woman took the baby into the forest, and her parents never saw their baby again.

The old woman called the baby Rapunzel. When Rapunzel grew up, the old woman locked her in a tall tower in the middle of the forest.

Every day the old woman came to bring her food.

"Rapunzel, Rapunzel, let down your hair!" she called, and Rapunzel let down her hair for the old woman to climb up. Every day was the same, and Rapunzel became very unhappy. She was a prisoner in the tower!

One day in the fall, a handsome young prince was passing by on his big black horse. He heard an old woman call, "Rapunzel, Rapunzel, let down your hair." He saw a beautiful young woman let down her long golden hair for the old woman to climb up.

"What a lovely girl, but she looks so sad," he thought. He waited until the old woman had gone away before going near the tower.

"Rapunzel, Rapunzel, let down your hair!" he called.

"Who are you?" asked Rapunzel.

"I'm a prince!" he answered. "Please let down your hair so I can come up and talk to you."

He looked kind, so Rapunzel let down her hair and the prince climbed up into the tower.

"Why are you a prisoner in this tower?" he asked her.

"I don't know," said Rapunzel. "The old woman keeps me here. I'm so lonely."

The prince visited Rapunzel every evening and she became happier and happier. Rapunzel fell in love with the kind, gentle prince and he quickly fell in love with her, too. Every evening they talked and laughed together and he told her stories about his palace.

"Please take me away from here," Rapunzel asked him. So they made a plan.

"Tomorrow I will bring a rope and you can climb down and escape," said the prince.

BUT the old woman was listening. She wanted to know why Rapunzel was happy and so came into the tower through a door at the bottom and hid there. Now she was angry. After the prince had left, she cut off Rapunzel's hair and locked her in a room at the bottom of the tower.

"You horrible girl!" she shouted at Rapunzel, "You wanted to escape from me! You will never escape, never!"

The old woman tricked the prince. She took Rapunzel's hair to the window and waited for the prince to come.

"Rapunzel, Rapunzel, let down your hair!" he called, and the old woman let down Rapunzel's hair for the prince to climb up. When he got to the top, the old woman let go of the hair.

"Arrgh!" the prince cried, falling down into a thorn bush at the bottom of the tower.

The prince was badly hurt. His legs were cut, his arms were cut, and he could not move from the bush. He just lay in the snow. Everything was dark. He could not see anything. He was blind!

"Help! Help!" cried the prince, but nobody helped him. The old woman was taking Rapunzel away, far, far away, from her prince.

He was left alone, lost in the forest in the middle of winter, without his Rapunzel.

The winter passed and the spring came. The prince found the way out of the forest. But he could not find Rapunzel. He went everywhere calling for her. He walked and walked, and he called and called,

"Rapunzel, my Rapunzel, where are you?" He did not look like a prince now. His clothes were torn and his hair was long.

Meanwhile, Rapunzel had managed to escape from the old woman and started looking for her prince.

One day, he heard the sound of a sad love song. Rapunzel had sung this song every day since she started looking for her prince.

"Rapunzel, my Rapunzel, where are you?" he cried. Rapunzel ran to him, crying as she held him in her arms.

"Oh, I love you," she said. As her tears fell on his eyes, they opened and he could see again.

"Rapunzel, my Rapunzel, I have found you at last!"

The prince took Rapunzel far away from the forest
and the tower to his beautiful palace. He promised to
go and find her mother and father right away.

He asked her, "Will you marry me?" She was so
happy.

"Oh yes," she said.

He soon found her parents, and they were all very
happy to be together again. In the summer, they got
married. They lived happily ever after.

ACTIVITIES

BEFORE YOU READ

1. Look at the cover of the book. Who can you see? What is she like?

2. Look at the first page of the book. How many people can you see?

3. Look at pictures in the story and find these people. Tick ✔ in the box when you find them.
   - ☐ an old woman
   - ☐ a beautiful young girl
   - ☐ a mother and a father
   - ☐ a prince
   - ☐ a baby

   Who do you think is a good person in the story?
   Who do you think is a nasty person in the story?
   How do you know who is good and who is nasty?

4. Look through the pictures. Try to find:
   - ☐ a cottage
   - ☐ a tower
   - ☐ a blind man
   - ☐ a garden
   - ☐ a forest
   - ☐ tears
   - ☐ some vegetables
   - ☐ some hair
   - ☐ a palace

5. Look at the pictures. What do you think happens in the story?

AFTER YOU READ

1. When did these events happen? Match them. Use the
   pictures to help you.

   a. The baby was born in the   summer
   b. The prince met Rapunzel in the   summer
   c. The prince went blind in the   fall
   d. Rapunzel and the prince got married   winter
      in the   spring
   e. The prince looked for Rapunzel in the

2. Make a story about the old woman after Rapunzel ran
   away.

3. "And they lived happily ever after..."
   Continue the story after the prince and Rapunzel got
   married. What was their life like?

4. Read the story out loud. Take turns to be the mother,
   the father, the old woman. Practice saying these
   sentences with feelings:

   ☐ "Oh, I love you" (You are in love)

   ☐ "No! Don't take our baby!" (You are very frightened)

   ☐ "Rapunzel, my Rapunzel, where are you?" (You are
      very tired)